Cameos in Colossians

Meditations from
Paul's Letter to the Colossians

Denis A. Wheado

ISBN: 978-1-78364-524-4

www.obt.org.uk

****

THE OPEN BIBLE TRUST
Fordland Mount, Upper Basildon,
Reading, RG8 8LU, UK

Cameos in Colossians

Contents

Introduction

Introduction

It has been said that the Church today desperately needs the message of Colossians because we live in an age where religious tolerance is the accepted norm. What do we mean by "religious tolerance"? Compromise creeping into the Church has weakened its witness and influence, so much so, that when we hear the phrase "one religion is as good as another" we fail to challenge it. Those who try to harmonise the best of all religions in an attempt to produce a superior religion where Jesus Christ is but one of many religious leaders are given a place, and a hearing! Even in some evangelical circles there is a danger of "diluting the faith" for fear of upsetting those who believe differently from ourselves, allowing non-Christian beliefs and practices to creep in, thereby weakening our witness and influence even further.

This publications is not, however, intended to be a verse-by-verse commentary on Paul's letter to the Colossians, for space would not allow such a detailed project. In any case, there are many good commentaries from eminent scholars available today without the need for an additional one! As its title suggests, only selected verses are taken to provide "cameos" which seek to make the Bible relevant to the present age. Such cameos are, of course, based on the message to the Colossians, but with the aim of meeting a *personal* need in the church today.

Denis Wheadon

Background to Colossians

Background to Colossians

The Church in Colossae

There is no record of how the church began in Colossae. We know that Paul did not start it, and neither did he visit it. According to Colossians 1:4 and 9, he had only heard of it, further confirmed in Colossians 2:1, by the fact that he had never met the believers there personally. Although he had heard of their faith in Christ Jesus and their love for all the saints, he had also heard of other things which disturbed him greatly, because they could have a destructive effect upon their ministry. So he wrote them a letter and this put the church and the city of Colossae on the map!

The City of Colossae

Colossae was a small, somewhat insignificant city, one of three situated in the beautiful Lycus valley about one hundred miles from the coastal city of Ephesus, in the Roman province of Asia. The other two cities, which were more prosperous than Colossae, were Laodicea and Hierapolis. There was a Christian congregation in each of the three cities, as confirmed by Paul in Colossians 4:13. Because of an important trade route passing through the area, it became a vital meeting point between the East and the West.

There was a time when, as a result of their strategic positions, all three cities were developing, expanding and becoming prosperous. Gradually, however, Colossae began to decline into what could only be described as a second rate city. This was mainly caused by the road from Pergamum, Thyatira and Sardis, where it joined up with the great trade route from Ephesus, being sited farther west at Laodicea, a prosperous new city. There was also a disastrous earthquake in that area in AD 60 (about the time Paul wrote this letter to the Colossians, although it would appear that he had not heard of it when he wrote the letter because he makes no reference to it) which could have been a contributing factor to the city's decline.

In spite of this decline, however, the church continued to flourish, up to a point! At least it was important enough to attract the attention of Paul. It is possible, though that Colossae itself might never have received a mention in the New Testament had it not been for the church there. There is certainly no reference to it in the Book of Acts, the history book of the New Testament. The city was located in an area which is now southwest Turkey, near Honaz, some thirty miles east of Denzili. Today the site is uninhabited.

In spite of no specific record, we can piece together the various accounts in the Acts and the Epistles which will give us a fair idea of how the Colossian church began. In chapters 19 and 20 of the Acts we read of Paul's three-year ministry in Ephesus, during which time "all the Jews and Greeks who lived in the province of Asia heard the word of the Lord" (Acts 19:10). This would no doubt have included the three cities of Laodicea, Hierapolis and Colossae.

It was during this ministry of Paul's in Ephesus that we know of two men from Colossae becoming Christians – Epaphras and Philemon. In Colossians 1:7 we are told that Epaphras was "a faithful minister of Christ" in Colossae, and was possibly a key figure in the founding of the church there. According to Colossians 4:13 we are further told that "he is working hard for you and for those at Laodicea and Hierapolis". So Epaphras exercised a ministry in all three cities in that area.

Then in Colossians 4:17 there is a reference to Archippus which connects us with Philemon. In verses 1 and 2 of the letter to Philemon Paul writes, "To Philemon our dear friend and fellow worker, to Apphia our sister, to Archippus our fellow-soldier and to the church that meets in your home". Later, in the same letter (verse 23), there is a reference to Epaphras sending greetings from Rome, where he is a "fellow prisoner in Christ Jesus" with Paul, to Philemon. Apphia was Philemon's wife and Archippus his son. We can safely assume, although it is not specifically stated, that Apphia was in fact Philemon's wife because she would not have been mentioned in the address (verse 2) on a domestic matter if it were not so. Likewise, although again not specifically stated, we can assume Archippus to be Philemon's son for the same reason. The reference in Colossians 4:17 suggests that Archippus was also the pastor of the church which met at Philemon's house.

The Letter to the Colossians

The Letter to the Colossians

It is generally agreed that Paul wrote his letter to the Colossians around AD 60 to AD 61 during his time of imprisonment in Rome (Acts 28:30-31). Also around this time he met Onesimus, the runaway slave belonging to Philemon. Having led Onesimus to the Lord, Paul then wrote a letter to Philemon begging him to forgive his slave and receive him back, not as a slave but as a brother in the Lord. It was again around this time that Epaphras came to Rome, concerned about the corruption in his church back in Colossae, and seeking Paul's help. It seems to have been a very busy period for Paul! So he wrote another letter, this time to the Colossians.

We know from Colossians 4:12-13, that Epaphras remained with Paul in Rome. But Colossians 4:7 would suggest that it was Tychicus who delivered the letter to Colossae, and possibly at the same time according to Ephesians 6:21, he delivered a letter to the Ephesians as well. It is interesting to note that there are many similarities in the two letters, to the Colossians and the Ephesians, but whilst the special emphasis in Ephesians is on the Church as the Body of Christ, in Colossians Paul places the emphasis on Christ Himself, the Head of the Body. Incidentally, the church at Colossae was probably only about five years old when Paul wrote this letter, so it was a comparatively young church. The church at Ephesus was a little older.

As explained in the *Introduction* it is not the purpose of this small booklet to give a verse-by-verse commentary of the letter to the Colossians. Suffice to say, the corruption creeping into the church at Colossae which prompted Epaphras to seek Paul's help was called "syncretism". This was a system of combining ideas from other philosophies and religions with Christian teaching. This was, to a point, understandable in such a young church which consisted of Greeks and Jews as well as the local Phrygians – a very cosmopolitan church indeed – but it undermined the purity of Christian truth, and that was totally unacceptable. Paul could not let it go unchallenged.

Here, then, was what we might call a dangerous cocktail of Eastern philosophy, Jewish legalism and Christian teaching; no wonder Paul felt the need to write to this little-known church, emphasizing the Headship of Christ in His Church, thereby drawing a faithful portrait of the Lord Jesus Christ in all His Supreme Glory, Majestic Dignity and Divine Deity. A careful study of this letter to the Colossians (using a good commentary) will show how Paul urged the church at Colossae of the need to take a fresh hold on Christ, on His complete supremacy and on to the fact that He is all sufficient. This was Paul's theme throughout his letter.

Cameos in Colossians

Cameos in Colossians

In one of my previous booklets published by The Open Bible Trust – *The Land of Spiritual Experience* – I wrote:

> One cannot commend too highly the importance of regular Bible study and meditation. Indeed, God Himself says to us "Listen carefully and take to heart all the words I speak to you" (Ezekiel 3:10). Unlike an ordinary book, which contains just words, the Bible is a living Book. Its words are very much alive. It is unique in this respect. These living words have transformed the lives of countless men and women down through the ages...

> When we read it, study it, meditate upon it, because it is God's living word, He really speaks to us through that word, for like the Book, it's Author is alive also! Now the

question is, if the Bible is different from any other book, should we not read it differently from any other book? And the answer, of course, is a definite yes! To *make the Bible relevant to our situation* (which differs from person to person, incidentally) and for it to fulfill its purpose, not only should we not read it as we would an ordinary book, but we must receive it into our hearts also – unlike any ordinary book. This means *putting into action what we have read...*

The "cameos" that follow are an attempt to make the Bible relevant to our situation today, thus assisting us in putting into action what we have read.

Colossians 1:9

We have not stopped praying for you and asking God to fill you with the knowledge of His will through all spiritual wisdom and understanding.

We can all take encouragement from the truth that no one is useless to God – we all have work to do for Him, however humble or mundane it may be. As we keep our lines of communication open between Him and us, through prayer and meditation on His word, and constant fellowship with His people, so He will reveal His will to us. When God calls us *personally*, whatever the task, He will equip us *personally*, too. But the question is often asked, how can we be sure of God's will? Or, as the Bible puts it, how might we be sure that God will "fill you with the knowledge of His will"?

Is it not true to say that the more we get to know a person the more we are able to understand him? Surely it is the same with God. The foundation upon which this knowledge is built is prayer, for as we pray for ourselves and for each other, so we will be filled with such knowledge. Notice the words of Paul, "We have not stopped praying for you and asking God to fill you with the knowledge of His will". Here is a perfect example of the need for prayer, the value of prayer, the urgency of prayer. It is only by keeping these lines of communication open that we will be able to hear Him when He calls us.

There will be no doubt in our minds when He does call as to what He wants us to do for him. His call is *personal*, and may vary greatly from our neighbour's calling. But, we may well say, we are not experienced or knowledgeable enough to do what He wants us to do! Moses had the same problem! So did a few others in the Scriptures – and since! It is an old truth, yet one that is still valid, that He who calls will also equip. As we have already said, when God calls us *personally*, whatever the task, He will equip us *personally*, too, by the power of the Holy Spirit.

There is a good example of this in the Old Testament, where Bezalel was "called" or "chosen" by God for a specific task. "Then the Lord said to Moses, 'See I have chosen Bezalel son of Uri ... and I have filled Him with the Spirit of God, with skill, ability and knowledge in all kinds of crafts'" (Exodus 31:1-3). There was no doubt in Bezalel's mind that He had been called by God and no doubt as to the task he was to perform for the Lord. So what excuse have we to give the next time God reveals His will to us, and shows us in some way what He wants us to do for Him? Here, surely, is a word of challenge as well as encouragement. In other words, we just don't have an excuse any more!

Now it is equally true to say that, as God calls us *personally* to work for Him, and as He also equips us *personally* for the task, then this is made possible only as our knowledge of His will increases *personally*. Our responsibility, then, is to daily seek to increase that knowledge. We are back to keeping our lines of communication constantly open between God and ourselves, taking our example from Paul who never "stopped praying for you and asking God to fill you with the knowledge of His will". But there is more. Remember, the knowledge that came to Bezalel was because he was filled with the Spirit of God, and so our knowledge of God's will comes "through all spiritual wisdom and understanding".

There is yet another dimension to all this, and it is thrilling to consider it. Our knowledge of God's will for us *personally* coming to us through His Spirit, will increase with our *personal knowledge of God Himself.* Now, that is thrilling, and is the subject of our next "cameo". So to our word of challenge, and our word of encouragement, we now add a word of responsibility.

Colossians 1:10

That you may live a life worthy of the Lord and may please Him in every good way: bearing fruit in every good work, growing in the knowledge of God.

There are four things recorded in this verse which emphasise our responsibility as Christians. Life is like a journey, and as we "walk" through it we have this responsibility to live a life that is worthy of the Lord. Quickly we realize that He has set us a very high standard. Nevertheless, it is a standard to which we must attain. We have heard it said of one who has been apprehended in a shady deal, who up to that time has appeared to have an unblemished record, that such an act is not worthy of him. His reputation has become tarnished. For the Christian there is the added responsibility to live a life worthy of the Lord, for if we are not careful we might bring His reputation into disrepute, to cause it to become tarnished by *our* actions.

This brings us to our second responsibility. As we continue on our journey through life, we must daily seek to please the Lord in every way, in everything we do, in everything we say, making ourselves worthy of the Lord and worthy to bear the name Christian. When we love someone we want to know him better day by day, whilst at the same time we want to please him in every way possible. If this is true in the natural realm, how much more so should it be in the spiritual realm. And by the things we do and say we also have the responsibility – the third one recorded in this verse – to bear fruit in every good work; that is, as we "walk" the Christian way, so we get others to "walk" with us by our constant and consistent testimony, living a life worthy of the Lord.

Conversely, we should ever be mindful of the words of Jesus in Matthew's version of the Sermon on the Mount, when He warned the disciples to "Watch out for false prophets ... By their fruit you will recognise them..." (Matthew 7:15-16). This is living a life totally unworthy of the Lord. So the advice given to us by the writer to the Hebrews is important because it will enable us to bear fruit in every good work and to live a life that is worthy of the Lord, if we observe it. "Through Jesus, therefore, let us continually offer to God a sacrifice of praise – the fruit of lips that confess his name. And do not forget to do good and to share with others, for with such sacrifices God is pleased" (Hebrews 13:15-16). We please God when we bear fruit.

Jesus, in the Sermon on the Mount, made a statement which is relevant to this matter of bearing fruit. He said, "Each tree is recognised by its own fruit. People do not pick figs from thorn bushes, or grapes from briers" (Luke 6:44). Here is a challenging word to professing Christians, and one we should recognise. Can you imagine what confusion would be caused if the laws of nature changed? We would never be certain of a particular fruit from a particular tree. What a ludicrous situation if we should go into an apple orchard and find only bananas growing there!

Yet so often, professing Christians cause just such confusion, create just such a ludicrous situation, in the minds of unbelievers, by producing fruit that is totally unexpected – yes, and sometimes unacceptable! Jesus Himself said that His Father will be glorified and we will be known as His disciples, if we bear much fruit (John 15:8). We must therefore take great care to produce only the kind of fruit one would expect from a Christian. What fruit, you may ask? Love, joy, peace, patience, kindness, goodness, faithfulness, gentleness, self-control – but how often have we failed to produce good fruit like this? This is the fruit of the Spirit (Galatians 5:22-23). One who allows the Holy Spirit to take control can only produce such fruit. If, therefore, every tree is known by its fruit, the big question of every professing Christian is this – by what fruit am I known?

Day by day, if we live the Christian life in the way the Lord requires of us, allowing the Holy Spirit to take control, others will recognise our fruit. They will "see Jesus in us", as the old hymn puts it, and will want to know more about the Saviour. They will want to learn the "secret" of a happy, joyful peaceful life in a trouble-torn world. This is being fruitful. Now the only way we can be sure of walking worthily of the Lord, and being fruitful at the same time, is to recognise our fourth responsibility as contained in this verse. We have already said that God calls us *personally* to work for Him, to bear fruit for Him. We have also said that He will equip us *personally* for the task, and that this is made possible only as our knowledge of His will increases *personally*. To this we now add what is perhaps the most important responsibility of them all. Every moment of every day we must seek to increase our knowledge of God. And the more we learn of Him the more worthily will we walk, the more fruitful will we become, the more we will please Him, the more we will learn of Him and so on. So when Paul says, "That you may live a life worthy of the Lord and may please Him in every way: bearing fruit in every good work, growing in the knowledge of God", he is describing a continuing process and a continuous experience. And because it is both continuing and continuous, there is no end to it.

Colossians 1:23

Continue in your faith, established and firm, not moved from the hope held out in the gospel. This is the gospel that you heard and that has been proclaimed to every creature under heaven.

Something that is often denied the world, but is the constant sacred possession of every true Christian, is the gift of hope. That is, a sure and certain hope for the future, not the candy floss type of hope in the world which can blow away by a change in direction of the political or economic wind! We are talking of a *sure* and a *certain* hope which never changes, and is as safe, secure and certain as the Author of that hope.

Think of it for a moment – a sure and certain hope for the future. Now that surely, and most definitely, is a very sacred possession indeed in an uncertain world; some would even say, a world without any real hope at all. And because we have this hope, we then have a sense of divine peace as well, which is also a very valuable possession to have in a world of worries such as ours. As we were saying in the previous "cameo", if we have the Saviour, then we also have the "secret" of a happy, joyful, peaceful life in a trouble-torn world.

It is logical to suppose that if we lose hope we also lose our sense of peace. We cannot have one without the other! That is why this verse from Colossians is so very important, for if we obey it to the letter (a way in which we should always obey the Bible commands that are intended for us), we will ensure that we will never lose hope. The first thing is to "Continue in your faith, established and firm". We cannot experience a sense of hope and a sense of peace if we blow hot one day, then blow cold the next! *Continue* is the important word, knowing that the faith in which we continue is established and firm – as we ourselves should be.

What is this faith? It is "being sure of what we hope for and certain of what we do not see" (Hebrews 11:1). So we are back to the *sure* and *certain* hope, the essence of faith, which leads us to the next part of our verse, "not moved from the hope held out in the gospel". The word "gospel" simply means good news, the good news that Jesus Christ is not a dead prophet from the past, but a living Saviour very much for the present – and the future! We neglect the Word of God at our peril, for here we find the truth concerning the Christian's true hope. Move away from it and we could lose hope, and quite a few other blessings as well!

The true hope of the gospel is the certain return of the living Saviour, the Lord Jesus Christ. True Christians have that hope and believe that gospel. This gives them their sense of inner peace. So let us be sure that we continue steadfastly with our faith and never move away from the truths of the gospel, risking the loss of our most sacred possessions.

What is more, the responsibility of every Christian we mentioned earlier, to please God by bearing fruit, applies here also. With reference to this gospel, Paul went on to remind the Colossians, as

God's Word reminds us today, that it has been "heard" and "proclaimed" – but by whom? By those who believe it, live by it, and who have not moved away from its truths. So we have this *sure* and *certain* hope also. We also have a sure and certain responsibility to share it with others, to bear fruit, to please God, to increase in our knowledge of Him, to live a life worthy of the Lord. And so it goes on and on! We are back to that on-going process and continuous experience again.

Colossians 2:6

Just as you received Christ Jesus as Lord, continue to live in Him, rooted and built up in Him, strengthened in the faith as you were taught, and over-flowing with thankfulness.

When we said earlier that life is like a journey, and that as we "walk" through it we have, as Christians, certain responsibilities, one of those responsibilities is to bear frit. As we "walk" the Christian way, so we get others to "walk" with us by our constant and consistent testimony, living a life worthy of the Lord. The *Authorised (King James) Version* of Colossians 2:6 says, "As ye have therefore received Christ Jesus the Lord so walk ye in Him". Whether we "walk in Him" or "continue to live in Him" the principle is still the same.

The Christian's daily walk, the way he lives his life, is important, for it marks out his true spiritual experience. It should be possible to tell a true Christian by the way he walks through life.

Perhaps it is rather trite to say this, but it is a fact well worth recognising. In the physical realm it is often possible to judge a person's aim or purpose by the way he walks. To amble along with no particular destination in mind, turning this way and that as the mood takes him, is a far cry from the one who sets out, head held high, with determination to reach his desired goal. It may be the slow measured plod of the policemen on the beat, or the quick, purposeful steps of the nurse hurrying through the ward. Speed is not of the essence, determination and destination is.

In similar vein, the true Christian cannot honour God if he has no spiritual purpose in life, if he has no sure and certain hope, if his testimony is not constant and consistent, if he is not living a life that is worthy of the Lord. A Christian cannot bear fruit and please God if he frequently changes spiritual direction as his moods change, one day on fire for the Lord, the next day adopting a couldn't-care-less attitude. A true Christian has a goal and an aim in life, to reach his heavenly home and honour his heavenly Father as he walks – to know where he is going and to honour God while he is going!

Of course, this is impossible in our own strength. Walking daily with the Lord in a way that is pleasing and acceptable to Him, continuing daily to live a life in Him that will bring honour to God, is conditional. It depends first of all upon our receiving and accepting and acknowledging Jesus Christ as Lord. It depends upon our faith being built on a sure foundation ("rooted … in Him") with a strong spiritual life constructed on that foundation ("built up in Him"). It depends upon our faith being strengthened daily as we live a life "over-flowing with thankfulness".

Jesus Christ gives purpose, an aim in life. He provides for us a goal with that sure and certain hope we talked about earlier. But only by receiving that daily power that He gives us, the daily strengthening of our faith, the daily increasing of personal knowledge of God Himself, are we able to achieve that aim, fulfil that purpose, and reach that goal.

Colossians 2:12-13

Having been buried with Him in baptism and raised with Him through your faith in the power of God, who raised Him from the dead. When you were dead in your sins and in the uncircumcision of your sinful nature, God made you alive with Christ. He forgave us all our sins.

There are three similar phrases which are found very close together in these two verses which are of great significance. They are, "buried with Him ... raised with Him ... alive with Christ", significant because they outline the logical sequence of events in the spiritual experience of the true Christian. In each of these events the Lord is involved, and we are involved with Him, as illustrated by the words, "with Him". So let us follow the sequence through.

First we must be "buried with Him" – this was the beginning of our spiritual experience when our evil and sinful nature died, and was buried, made possible because Jesus Himself had passed that way before, yet without sin. A sinful nature, when it dies, needs to be buried just as a physical body, when it dies, needs to be buried – it is no longer of any use!

It is a comforting thought, and praise God a true one, that the whole of a Christian's life, past present and future, is bound up in the Lord Jesus Christ. In another of his letters Paul wrote, "For from Him and through Him and to Him are all things. To Him be the glory for ever! Amen" (Romans 11:36). So to our three significant phrases in Colossians we can now add three more from Romans, "From Him … through Him … to Him", again significant because in each the Lord is involved, and we are involved with Him.

Now, the Word says of the *past*: "From Him … are all things"; not only back at the beginning of time when He created the worlds, as we are reminded in John 1:3, - "Through him all things were made; without Him nothing was made that has been made", nor later, when He created you and me; not even His guiding hand all through the history of mankind, important though that has been. No, the most significant and vital event of all from the past, and certainly the one that has had the greatest effect upon the lives of men and women and young people down through the ages, is what occurred nearly two thousand years ago on a hill outside Jerusalem.

When Jesus purchased our salvation with the shedding of His own life's blood on the Cross of Calvary, and God His Father set the seal of approval upon that sacrifice three days later by raising His Son from the dead, God's supreme purpose was accomplished. All that had gone before, and all that was to follow this one great event, are "from Him". In fact, we can say all that has happened to us and for us and in us in the past, including being "buried with Him" is "from Him". All our past is bound up in the Lord Jesus Christ.

If we are honest with ourselves, we are *where* we are today and *what* we are today because of our Lord Jesus Christ, and His great provision in the past for our every need. But this is all bound up in the *present*, too. That is why, here and now in the present, because of the past, we can and must live our lives according to His word, because "through Him … are all things". A committed Christian can only live his life fully, acceptable unto God his Heavenly Father, with a deep sense of spiritual satisfaction (not a very satisfactory word, for a Christian can never be really satisfied!) through the Lord Jesus Christ. He is here in the present to help us, to guide us, to inspire and empower us. No dead prophet here, only a living Saviour, because Jesus is alive!

So the next logical step is to be "raised with Him". As a result of our new birth we can come out of death (that is, our dead sinful nature, the death of our old self, where we were "buried with Him") into a new life. This phrase, "a new birth", is just another name for spiritual conversion. It is based on the words of Jesus to Nicodemus. "I tell you the truth, no-one can see the kingdom of God unless he is born again" (John 3:3). But this is only the beginning.

Some people try to live their lives as if Jesus was dead, thereby denying any power the risen Saviour is waiting to bestow through His Holy Spirit. One day, many years ago, at the conclusion of a weekend conference in the Christian hotel we owned before our retirement, a lady came into my office, just prior to departure, on the pretext that she was offended by the "Jesus stickers" on the mustard-pots. This was an idea suggested by a younger member of the hotel staff who, herself, knew the truth of the words, *Jesus is alive!* The circular stickers fitted the covers of the mustard pots just perfectly! Not wanting to discourage spiritual initiative I had agreed to their use.

The lady started by saying, "I don't want to be reminded that Jesus is alive when I am putting mustard on my roast beef." I felt led to ask her if she herself really believed that He was alive; if she had ever fully committed her life to the Lord, living every day close to a *living* Saviour; if, in fact, she was a Christian. Her reply was immediate. "I go regularly to church every Sunday." "With respect," I replied, "I didn't ask if you went to church. I asked you if you were a *Christian.*"

One of the blessings of salvation is the assurance of the Holy Spirit that we are children of God, that we are truly saved, that we know our sins are forgiven, that we have been adopted into the Family of God. Her reply presented an opportunity for me to witness to her of a living Saviour. Being a Christian is not something we *think* we are, but something we *know* we are. There should be no doubt. The fact that this lady had been offended by "Jesus stickers" on the mustard pots said a lot for her spiritual experience – or lack of it! Thank God, I was able to tell her from personal experience of a *living* Saviour, One who lives with me every minute of every day.

When she left the office, after quite a long time, I cannot say she had made any open confession of salvation, but I believe God the Holy Spirit would continue to work in her heart and life, so that she would not be offended by the reminder that Jesus is alive the next time she put mustard on her roast beef (or at any other time, for that matter) – because the Bible says of the present "through Him … are all things". And because He is alive we can now be "risen with Him".

But what of the *future*? Can we be sure of that? Can we be certain that He will be there, too? The Word says, "to Him are all things." Everything from the past, through the present, points towards the future, when He will fulfil His promise to come again and receive us unto Himself. "For from Him and through Him and to Him are all things". The culmination of all things are in Him in the future, which according to world events at the present moment may not be far away!

Now this phrase can only be a comfort to us if we are prepared to accept it as being true, and live according to it day by day. The sure and certain hope we are talking about earlier, bringing with it a sure and certain sense of peace, can be ours if we live every moment of every day in the *present*, realising this is made possible by what has happened for us and to us in the *past*, and if we live our lives in the light of Christ's return for His own in the *future*. We will derive comfort, hope and peace from the fact that everything concerning us is bound up in the Lord Jesus Christ.

So the next stage in our spiritual experience is a continuing one, a daily experience, a moment by moment experience, for we are "alive with Christ". Our new life is lived in and through Jesus made more alive by the One with whom we were buried, then raised, and now made alive with daily spiritual vitality. All this may sound very complicated, whereas it is really quite simple. It can be summed up in three words – death, resurrection and life. The death of our sinful life, the resurrection to a new life in Christ, and the daily living of that new life.

This is the logical sequence of events in the spiritual experience of all true Christians. What could be simpler? "For from Him and through Him are all things" – as we are His! Or are we offended by the mustard pot stickers?

Colossians 3:2

Set your minds on things above, not on earthly things.

There are many references throughout the Scriptures which illustrate the contrast between "things above" and "earthly things". Perhaps the most well known is in the Sermon on the Mount, where Jesus said, "Do not store up for yourselves treasures on earth, where moth and rust destroy, and where thieves break in and steal. But store up for yourselves treasures in heaven, where moth and rust do not destroy, and where thieves do not break in and steal" (Matthew 6:19-20). Now these verses teach us more than the assurance that there will be no moths, rust or thieves in heaven! The next verse gives us the "punch line", and echoes our verse from Colossians at the same time. "For where your treasure is, there your heart will be also" (Matthew 6:21). Or, as Paul puts it, "Set your minds on things above, not on earthly things."

When we consider these statements they are really very simple yet so very profound. One might logically suppose that where our heart is there lies our affection also. The boy who has lost his heart to a particular girl will tell you where *his* affection lies! This matter of the affection of the heart is not a new phenomenon, even though some modern pop songs would have us believe they have discovered something new. Solomon, in his great love poem, experienced it. "You have stolen my heart with one glance of your eyes, with one jewel of your necklace" (Song of Songs 4:9). So the heart and affection are synonymous. No wonder Jesus used it as a pointer to where our true affection really lies. Store up treasure in heaven, not on the earth. Where your treasure is, there is where your heart is also, says Jesus. Paul takes up the theme. So set your mind on the place where your treasure is, not on earthly things, he says. *The Authorised (King James) Version* renders this verse, "Set your affection on things above, not on things on the earth." For the Christian the situation is very similar to that of the young lover. He seeks only to please his loved one. He loves her with every fibre of his being. Now translate that from the emotional to the spiritual.

A true Christian seeks only to please his Lord, to build up spiritual wealth or treasure, to love God with every fibre of his being. His is a love which involves his emotions, his motives, his knowledge, just as Jesus commanded. Taking an Old Testament command, Jesus reinvested it with a new meaning. "Love the Lord your God with all your heart and with all your soul and with all your mind and with all your strength" (Mark 12:30). So our consideration must always be "on things above", upon the eternal, rather than "on earthly things", those which are temporal.

Let us digress for a moment and look at this Old Testament command re-emphasised by Jesus. His greater revelation of Almighty God as a loving Heavenly Father reveals just how we should love Him – "with all your heart". This involves our emotions and affects how we *feel* about Him. "With all your mind" governs our knowledge, and dictates how much we *learn* about Him. "With all your strength" has to do with our whole physical being, showing how much we desire to *serve* Him.

If we acknowledge our love for God as Jesus here commands us to do, and in the way that He commands it too, then that love will be acceptable unto Him. Why? How can we be sure? Because it involves emotions, our motives, our knowledge, indeed, our whole being; what we might say, a complete and total love for God, a complete setting of our mind (our affections) on things above. But this is only the half of it!

Jesus went on to say, "Love your neighbour as yourself. There is no commandment greater than these" (Mark 12:31). The quality of our love for God affects, controls, governs, dictates our love for our neighbour, whether that neighbour lives on the continent of Africa or of America, or right next door in Britain (or anywhere else where we happen to live). And God knows we could certainly do with a lot more love in the world right now! This love for our neighbour will support our responsibility, mentioned earlier, to bear fruit.

We also said earlier that life is like a journey, and that as we "walk" through it we have, as Christians, certain responsibilities, one of which is to bear fruit. As we "walk" the Christian way, so we get others to "walk" with us by our constant and consistent testimony, living a life worthy of the Lord. But we will never get our neighbour to "walk" with us unless we show a God-like love towards him. Our daily witness, our daily "walk", the way we act and think and speak, will demonstrate to us personally, to those around us as well as to the Lord Himself, just where our affections really lie, where our treasure is stored.

Paul is very simple in his statement. "Set your minds on things above, not on earthly things." It will have its effect upon ourselves as well as others. If there are any doubts in our mind right now, then we need to examine our experience, for a true Christian has no doubt about his affections, and his treasure – he knows *exactly* where they lie, where they are stored. Here is another challenge facing us.

Colossians 3:15

Let the peace of Christ rule in your hearts, since as members of one body you were called to peace. And be thankful.

This most important and valuable gift of peace, so very necessary in this trouble-torn world, is, as most of us have to confess with the hymn writer, something so often forfeited. "O what peace we often forfeit, O what needless pain we bear," he writes. In an earlier "cameo" we said that something that is often denied the world, but is the constant sacred possession of every true Christian, is the gift of hope. Then we said, because we have this hope, we have a sense of divine peace as well, a valuable possession in a world of worries, as ours is. If we have the Saviour, then we also have the "secret" of a happy, joyful, peaceful life – and this in spite of the fact that we do live in a trouble-torn world.

Now, if this is all true, why do we sometimes seem to forfeit this valuable gift of peace? A closer study of Paul's words here to the Colossians will help us to a clearer understanding of what we mean by "the peace of Christ" and thereby help us to safeguard against forfeiting it. Christian peace is the gift of God's love, not something we obtain through our own efforts. It is not dependent upon circumstances surrounding us, but upon our experience within us. The moment we gave our heart to the Lord we should, if the experience was genuine, have begun from that moment to enjoy peace *with* God and know, too, the peace *of* God. No one can take it away. It is God's free gift to us.

Yet we still have to admit that there are times when we really do forfeit this gift of peace. Why should this be? The answer is two-fold, and both are contained in our verse. Notice what Paul says. "Let the peace of Christ *rule* in your hearts." First of all, then, we have to realise that God's peace must rule, be in complete control, must take over. We do not control our inner peace, God does! It is subject to God's laws. When we obey His will, acknowledge His rule as King of our lives, then we have lasting peace. When Paul said earlier, "Continue in your faith" (1:23) he meant just that!

We cannot experience a sense of hope and a sense of peace if we blow hot one day, then blow cold the next! *Continue* is the important word. Likewise, we will forfeit our gift of peace if we allow God to rule as King one day, then we take control of our lives the next. *Continue* is still the important word here.

Secondly, notice again what Paul says. "Let the peace of God rule in your *hearts*." There is something specific and definite in this statement. He does not say that the peace of Christ should rule our heads, or our minds, or anywhere else we please. He says specifically, Christ's peace must rule in our *hearts*, the centre of our inner self, the central control of our whole spiritual being. It is here where peace must rule, must be in complete control.

The storms of life may roar around us, but if we are sure that the Giver of all perfect gifts rules in our hearts, then we may be sure that His gifts rule too. One such precious gift is His perfect peace. But only if we let the peace of Christ rule in our hearts in the first place. But only if we let the peace of Christ rule in our hearts in the first place can we be sure of not forfeiting that peace. The onus is on us!

Colossians 3:16: The Word of Christ

Let the Word of Christ dwell in you richly as you teach and admonish one another with all wisdom.

In the previous "cameo" we spoke about the peace of Christ ruling within us. Now we consider the Word of Christ dwelling within us, or as we sometimes use the phrase, God's Word. Paul hints strongly here at the richness of God's Word. Sometimes it almost overwhelmed him, as he expressed it in Romans 11:33, "Oh, the depth of the riches of the wisdom and knowledge of God!" We learn of the wisdom and knowledge of God through His Word. And because of its richness, Paul encourages us to use it to "teach and admonish one another with all wisdom". As he reminded Timothy concerning the Scriptures, it "is useful for teaching, rebuking, correcting and training in righteousness" (2 Timothy 3:16).

But Paul never lost sight of the fact that what he wrote were not *his* words. The emphasis upon teaching and preaching and admonishing was not according to what *he* said. Notice again whose word is to dwell in us richly and from which we should teach and preach. It is the Word of *Christ.* All through his life, following his encounter with Jesus on the Damascus Road, Paul was consistent in his emphasis – Christ Jesus first and last, and all points in between! At the very beginning of his public ministry we read, "At once he began to preach in the synagogues that Jesus is the Son of God" (Acts 9:20). From the beginning he was setting the example of letting the Word of Christ dwell in him richly so that through his ministry he was able to encourage others to do the same. Let us pause for a moment and look at this simple statement, yet one that teaches us two very important lessons as it illustrates Paul's word to the Colossians of letting the Word of Christ dwell in us richly.

Here was a young man who, as yet, was still called Saul (It was not until Acts 13:9 that he was called Paul). He had just become what we today would call a Christian. (It was not until Acts 11:26 that the word Christian was actually used). Here was a new convert, and what did he do? Did he preach the Church? No! Although, until recently he had set out with Jewish authority to persecute the Church. Saul had been a religious Jew, so did he preach his own ideas based on his religious upbringing? Again, no! The Word of God says he preached *Jesus*. He was letting the Word of Christ dwell in him richly.

"Salvation is found in no one else, for there is no other name under heaven given to men by which we must be saved" (Acts 4:12). That name was Jesus, of course, as the context of Peter's words reveals. And Saul took up the theme. What a lesson we can learn from this convert! Whenever we preach, whether in word or in deed, whenever we teach or admonish in wisdom, let it always be in the name of Jesus Christ. So often today we hear ideas preached from the pulpit which make us wonder in whose name the preacher is preaching. In recent days we have actually heard the pulpit used for preaching politics, setting the National

Health Service to right, and a host of other non-Christian topics!

Permit a personal reference. I can truthfully say that, in all my years of ministry (pushing on towards half a century now!), I have never preached any other name than that of Jesus Christ, and I have always found as a safeguard the maxim: "Preach only what the Bible says!" Indeed, one of my books actually has the title, "*Good Morning ... The Bible Says*". Too many people today preach either what they think the Bible says, or worse still, what they think it ought to say! As we said in the *Introduction*, it has been said that the Church today desperately needs the message of Colossians because we live in an age when religious tolerance is the accepted norm. We tolerate, and allow to go unchallenged, preaching that is suspect. We should beware and take an example from Paul. The Bible says of him, "at once he began to preach ... Jesus."

But look at that sentence again, for there is another valuable lesson contained in it. "*At once* he began to preach ... Jesus." Maybe you have met some

Christians who sit and think about effective witness, who meet and plan for effective witness, then continue to sit and think and plan! They never get anything done! Whether a new convert, or one who has travelled the Christian way for many years, the time to sit and think and plan has gone. The need for the hour is to preach Jesus, and to set about it at once. "Never put off to tomorrow what can be done today" still holds good when applied to preaching Jesus to the people.

There is a delightful story told by the late J. D. Drysdale of Birkenhead, England, and quoted in his book *Holiness in the Parables*. He tells of a young convert who was asked if he had done anything for Christ since he had believed.

"Oh, I am a learner," he replied.
"Well, when you light a candle, do you do it to make the candle more comfortable, or to give light?" his friend asked.
"To give light, of course."
"Do you expect it to give light after it has half burned, or when you first light it."
"As soon as I light it."

"Very well; go and do likewise; begin at once!"

Shortly after, Drysdale tells us, there were fifty more Christians in that town as a result of that young man's testimony.

The Bible says, immediately he became a Christian (as we would say today), Saul began preaching Jesus. No hesitation, no delay no putting it off to another day – the message was urgent. It still is urgent today! *At once* he began to preach ... Jesus. At once he began to preach ... *Jesus.*

But it all began for Saul (Paul), and continued all through his ministry and his letters, when he "let the word of Christ dwell in (him) richly". It will begin and continue through our Christian "walk" when we "let the word of Christ dwell in (us) richly". The priority and urgency of that word is highlighted by this important phrase. But it highlights another important truth, as well as illustrating the consistency of Paul's preaching, as we shall see in our next "cameo".

Colossians 3:16: Gratitude

Let the word of Christ dwell in you richly ... as you sing psalms, hymns and spiritual songs with gratitude in your hearts to God.

We said earlier that through all his life, following his encounter with Jesus on the Damascus road, Paul was consistent in his emphasis – Christ Jesus first and last, and all points in between! Notice here the effects yet again of letting the Word of Christ dwell in us richly. Not only does it reveal the priority of teaching and admonishing one another with all wisdom, of the priority and urgency of preaching in the name of Jesus only, but it also reveals the importance of praise – a natural transition from preaching to praise here in one verse.

To further illustrate the consistency of Paul's ministry, we can turn to another one of his letters, where he wrote, "Be filled with the Spirit. Speak to one another with psalms, hymns and spiritual songs. Sing and make music in your heart to the Lord, always giving thanks to God the Father for everything, in the name of our Lord Jesus Christ" (Ephesians 5:18-20). We said in an earlier "cameo" that some people try to live their lives as if Jesus was dead, thereby denying any power the risen Saviour is waiting to bestow through His Holy Spirit. We must not underestimate the power of the Holy Spirit, nor ignore the purpose of His presence, which is why we find the Third Person of the Trinity linked to our paean of praise.

There are two very important things suggested by our verse here from Colossians, linked to the verses in Ephesians. Firstly, our Christian "walk" with the Lord should be a *joyful* one, and secondly it should be a *thankful* one. As we look at these two aspects a little more closely, notice that they are a direct result of being filled with the Spirit and letting the Word of Christ dwell in us richly.

If we have allowed the Spirit to indwell and fill us daily, and if the Word of Christ really does dwell in us richly, then the evidence will show through a *joyful life*. This is not to say that there will never come a time when we are sad or upset. Anyone who suggests that becoming a Christian means we will never suffer, never be frustrated, will always be immune to all the cares and worries of this life, is just not telling the truth. If, on the other hand, our lives are Spirit-filled and Christ's Word is dwelling in us richly, what a difference it will make when those cares do come along, as they no doubt will. We will be able to face our suffering *together* with the Lord.

Nor does it mean, of course, that we walk around all day with a permanent grin on our face, rather like a pious Cheshire cat! The joy that comes with the indwelling of God's Spirit and God's Word, is a deep-seated, lasting joy. Naturally it will show in our faces, in our actions, and in our very attitude to life. There will be a natural joy which will express itself in many ways, and at all times. What is more natural than wanting to express our joy in singing "psalms, hymns and spiritual songs"?

Allow me to illustrate this with another reference to the Christian Hotel from which we have now retired. During the twenty-two years we were there, hardly a day went by when at some time through the working hours guests and staff could be heard singing "psalms, hymns and spiritual songs" somewhere in the building. During one of the Sunday Night Fellowship Hours, a regular feature of the hotel when the guests (and often the staff) would get together to share their blessings through testimony and singing, one guest testified to the fact that when he had arrived for his holiday just over a week before, he had lost the joy of the Lord in his life. He went on to confess that he still knew the Lord as his Saviour, he still loved the Lord, he still acknowledged God as his Heavenly Father, he still took an active part in the church back home and he would still classify himself as a born-again Christian. But somehow all the joy of Christian living had gone out of his life. That night in the lounge he was praising God because he had re-discovered the joy of the Lord. I suppose we could say that he had allowed the Holy Spirit to flood his soul, he had allowed the Word of Christ to dwell in him richly. But what had caused this to happen?

During the week he had already spent at the hotel he had noticed the happy way in which the staff went about their work. This had set him thinking. Then one morning, before setting off across the road to the beach, a little later than usual, he heard one of the girls praising the Lord in song. He followed the sound of her voice, particularly attracted by the sincerity of the melody, and was amazed when he found what she was doing.

"I went back to my room," he confessed, "knelt by my bed, and asked the Lord to forgive me. As I prayed I felt the joy of the Lord returning. That girl was praising the Lord *as she was cleaning the toilets*! How ashamed I was. If she was able to praise the Lord doing a menial task like that, how much more should I be praising the Lord for all His goodness to me right now as I enjoy this wonderful holiday." There is really nothing more we can add to that!

If we have allowed the Spirit to indwell and fill us daily, and if the Word of Christ really does dwell in us richly, then the evidence will also show through a *thankful life*. Every moment of every day we should be able to find something for which to thank the Lord. Indeed every born-again Christian has the greatest thing for which he can thank God – his salvation.

When we received Jesus Christ as our Saviour it opened up such a wealth of spiritual blessings from our Heavenly Father that we need never cease to thank Him. Think just for a moment where we might have been today but for the Lord; pause and consider all the spiritual riches that we possess right now. In the words of the hymn-writer, "Count your many blessings, name them one by one, and it will surprise you what the Lord has done." Or perhaps the "alternative version" would be even more appropriate. "Count your many blessings, name them by the score, and it will surprise you there are thousands more!" Yes, there is much for which we can thank our Heavenly Father.

Many years ago I travelled to Yorkshire in the North of England to conduct some Anniversary Services in a town where I had been responsible, with my wife, for the Lord's work several years before that. During my visit I went to see an old lady who was now confined to one room in her home. Suffering with a bad heart and crippled with arthritis, it was all she could do to hobble from her bed to a chair by the window. Even the slightest effort would result in her gasping for breath. She had been very poorly years before as a member of my congregation; she was now very much worse. I was shocked at her deteriorated condition.

One thing she used to say quite often whenever I visited her, and she was still saying it when I visited her again that anniversary weekend, really humbled me. "I have so much to thank God for," she would say. "I have Him, I have Jesus, I have His Spirit and I'm alive!" And she meant it! The purpose of my visits were to help and encourage her spiritually myself. By comparison, I had so much more for which to thank God. She always taught me a valuable lesson in simple thanksgiving, for she was "always giving thanks to the Father for everything, in the name of our Lord Jesus Christ".

The Bible enumerates many ways whereby we can be sure that we are filled with the Spirit of God, that we have let the Word of Christ dwell in us richly. In our verse here from Colossians Paul has highlighted two – *joyfulness:* "as you sing psalms, hymns and spiritual songs"; and *thankfulness:* "with gratitude in your hearts to God the Father for everything". So the questions we need to ask ourselves are, do we know something of spiritual joy in our lives? Are we always thankful to the Lord for His goodness toward us? If we can truthfully answer "yes", then we can be sure we have been "filled with the Spirit" and that we have "let the word of Christ dwell in (us) richly".

Colossians 3:17

Whatever you do, whether in word or deed, do it all in the name of the Lord Jesus, giving thanks to God the Father through Him.

It is vitally important how, as Christians, we speak and act, for when we take upon ourselves the noble name of *Christian* we take with it the responsibility of speaking and acting for the Lord Himself. Indeed, this was how the first disciples received, what was originally a nickname, but also a name carrying heavy responsibilities, in the city of Antioch. In one of my other booklets published by The Open Bible Trust – *In My Father's Hose* – I wrote:

> The Bible tells us that the disciples were first called Christians in the city of Antioch (Acts 11:26), where, as a result of bearing much fruit, as commanded by Jesus, they were quickly noticed by the population of the city and were readily given a nickname which

has come down through the centuries an honourable name.

Paul is here saying to the Colossians, and through His Word God is saying to us, "Whatever you do, whether in word or deed, do it all in the name of the Lord Jesus." In other words, we must live so that our lives will be quickly noticed by those around us and readily earn the name Christian, as did the disciples in Antioch. But what was so significant about these men? Answering that question may well help us to an understanding of what Paul means here.

Again quoting from *In My Father's House*

At first sight there is nothing very significant in those disciples receiving this name. They could have been called Christians first in Jerusalem or Bethlehem, or even Nazareth. It is only when we realise the kind of city that Antioch really was that we begin to see the importance of the situation. It was a city of low moral standards, where idol worship was normal, where true spiritual standards virtually did not exist.

Yet here, in a sordid, depraved, degrading society, a group of people stood out sufficiently by the way they lived their lives, recognised as very different by their attitude towards each other, as well as towards others around them, that they earned for themselves this special name. It paid tribute to a people so unlike those around them as to be noticed. They were not swallowed up in the mire of immoral living. In short, they were different.

Their difference was not denominational. It was not racial. It was a quality of living, a dynamic witness, a perfect example of bearing much spiritual fruit, which, in New Testament terms, can be called *faith*. As a result of that faith, their attitude toward God, toward each other, and toward those outside their own particular community who needed Christ, was such that the Bible records the fact that "the disciples were called Christians first in Antioch". The big question now is, of course, what do people call us just where we live?

This is a very important question and needs to be answered. As we have already said, when we take upon ourselves the name of Christian we must take the responsibility that goes with it. Unfortunately, this is not always the case, and is the reason why sometimes Christians attract justifiable criticism – they accept the name but do not accept the responsibility that goes with it! A true Christian should seek to speak and act as if the Lord Himself has spoken or acted. This is why it is so necessary to not only observe Paul's words here, but to obey them also. "Whatever you do, whether in word or deed, do it all in the name of the Lord Jesus." In another of his letters Paul says, "Whatever you do, do it all for the glory of God" (1 Corinthians 10:31).

A true Christian's responsibility, then is to be a true reflection of his Lord in every way, in word and deed, in the name of the Lord, bringing glory to God. If we continually ask ourselves these two questions in every situation, "What would Jesus say?" and "What would Jesus do?" we are halfway to accepting our full responsibility. The other half, of course, is actually saying and doing as Jesus would! Then having discharged our responsibility faithfully, we can go on to obey the second half of the verse, "giving thanks to God the Father through him (Jesus)". Notice again the consistency of Paul's preaching and teaching. He has already emphasised in an earlier verse that our Christian walk" with the Lord should be a joyful one and a thankful one.

Giving thanks to God is a theme to which Paul returns time and time again in his letters. Already in Colossians we have noticed this recurring theme. "Overflowing with thankfulness" (2:6); "And be thankful" (3:15); "With gratitude in your heart to God" (3:16); "Giving thanks to God the Father" (3:17). So let us day by day discharge our responsibility faithfully, then we can go on to praise the Lord by giving thanks, by being thankful, by overflowing with thankfulness, and so we could go on. But it all begins with recognising and accepting our full responsibility in the first place, then the rest will follow quite naturally.

Colossians 4:2
Prayer

Devote yourselves to prayer, being watchful and thankful.

The theme of thankfulness continues, this time linked with prayer, which is also a recurring theme in Paul's letters. Many good books have been written on the subject of prayer. However, one or two brief observations on this all important aspect of a Christian's experience have their place here. Paul's consistency in his letters was recognised by the apostle Peter when he said, "Our dear brother Paul also wrote to you with the wisdom that God gave him. He writes the same way in all his letters" (2 Peter 3:15-16). So references to prayer throughout his letters do not surprise us. Here he is saying that we should devote ourselves to prayer; to the Ephesians he wrote, "pray in the Spirit on all occasions with all kinds of prayers" (Ephesians 6:18); to the Thessalonians he wrote, "pray continually" (1 Thessalonians 5:16); and in almost all his letters Paul makes some reference to his own prayers for others.

In an earlier "cameo" we highlighted *joyfulness* and *thankfulness* as two evidences of being filled with the Spirit of God and letting the word of Christ dwell in us richly. We could have gone on to highlight *prayerfulness* as a powerful evidence, too. It is only through prayer that we are able to keep in touch with the Source of our joy; only through prayer can we keep in touch with the Person to whom we are thankful. So Paul knew what he was writing when he said to the Colossians, "devote yourselves to prayer", and to the Ephesians, "always keep on praying", and to the Thessalonians, "pray continually".

But how is it possible to pray *continually*? Very easily when we realise and understand the true nature of prayer – keeping in touch constantly with the Lord. In other words, divine communion is a form of prayer, and such communion with God for a true Christian is *continuous,* never ending. And another thing, not all prayers are said in church, nor at our bedside. I well remember some very valuable prayer sessions on a bicycle back in the 1950's, riding across the hills along a quiet country road every Sunday afternoon for two years to conduct a Sunday school in County Durham, England. I think too, of the little old lady in an old people's home in Yorkshire who would sit for hours in a crowded room with her apron over her head talking with the Lord, cut off completely from her surroundings.

My own experience is such that I include the Lord in my conversations, talking with Him as if he were actually there – as indeed He is! I suppose it would be true to say that much of our praying is done without thinking we are praying, in the sense that God is automatically brought into our lives on a day to day basis, and has become part of our very existence. We are, of course, back to this matter of divine communion, devoting ourselves to prayer, praying continually.

It is interesting to note that after Paul encourages us to devote ourselves to prayer, in the next verse he says, "And pray for us, too" (4:3), suggesting what another apostle specifically states, "pray for each other" (James 5:16). There are two very important reasons why we should pray for each other, for it reminds us that our prayers must not be selfish and self-centred. When we pray for one another, our care, our concern, our love for others will increase. This is the first reason, and why Jesus commanded us to "Love your enemies and pray for those who persecute you" (Matthew 5:44). When we pray for another, especially if he or she has been unkind or particularly hurtful to us, we cannot hate that person or even dislike him. Our attitude must change. It can do no other! Many of our petty thoughts and jealousies will disappear when we learn to pray like this.

The second reason is exactly the opposite! When we pray for another, our care, our concern, our love for ourselves will decrease. How often do we become so absorbed with our own personal affairs, our own considerations and circumstances, that we have no time or thought for others? It is possible even to relegate God to second place in such a situation. We must come first! The great capital "I" must be above everything! A dangerous situation indeed! Whilst

God does not expect us to exclude ourselves completely from our prayers, at least a proper balance should be maintained. We shall have less time for self when we devote our prayers to the needs of others. The children's chorus – J.O.Y. – is never more true than in this: "Jesus first, Yourself last, and Others in between".

Here then is a clear command which we must obey if we are to live a full Christian life, and for two very good reasons, too. We must learn to pray for each other. And one other thought concerning prayer before we move to the next "cameo", Jesus also said, "whatever you ask for in prayer, believe…" (Mark 11:24), or as the *Authorised (King James) Version* renders it, "when ye pray, believe". There are two delightful little stories, both involving rain, which illustrate the truth of these words. It is futile to devote ourselves to prayer, to pray continually, and not believe at the same time that God hears and answers those prayers, even though the answer may sometimes be "no!" Indeed we should be prepared for "no" answers, they are just as important as the positive ones.

n the eve of the Sunday School outing the pastor realised that they had forgotten to personally invite Mrs. Brown, a very difficult member of the church at the best of times. So he dashed to her house to correct the omission.

"It's too late," she retorted.
"I don't understand," the pastor replied. "Have you made other plans, then?"
"No, I'm stopping at home."
The pastor was puzzled. "Then why is it too late?" he asked.
The old lady glared straight at him. "Because I have already prayed for rain and I don't want to get wet!"
"Whatever you ask for in prayer, believe…"

Then there was the group of people who decided to meet in the church one evening to pray for rain because of a terrible drought in their area. There had been no rain for several months and everyone was suffering badly as a result One of the group turned up to pray with an umbrella over his arm. The others began to ridicule him.

"The sun has shone for months, it has shone all day today, there's not a cloud in the sky," they scoffed.

Then they were all put to shame by his reply. "We are going to pray for rain, surely we must believe our prayers are going to be answered. If not, why are we here? I believe, so I have come prepared. I don't want to get wet going home!"

"Whatever you ask for in prayer, believe..."

There is nothing more to add to these two little stories except to say, "When ye pray, believe."

Colossians 4:7: Tychicus

Tychicus … he is a dear brother, a faithful minister and fellow servant in the Lord.

A basic definition of being a Christian is not someone who attends church regularly, nor yet someone who lives an honest and good life, although these things are very commendable and should form part of a true Christian's way of life. But they do not form part of any definition. A true definition of a Christian is one who has a personal *relationship* with God through Christ. This matter of relationship is important in the Christian life, not only to God but to our fellow Christians as well, and is emphasised very strongly in this verse concerning Tychicus.

The description Paul gives of this young man should be that of every true Christian; "a dear brother" describes his relationship to his fellow Christians. This is why we so often hear believers in a local church refer to each other as brothers and sisters in the Lord. Indeed, Paul enjoins us in another of his letters to "be devoted to one another in brotherly love" (Romans 12:10). This relationship to fellow-Christians is further emphasised by Paul when writing to the Thessalonians. "Now about brotherly love we do not need to write to you, for you yourselves have been taught by God to love each other. And in fact, you do love all the brothers throughout Macedonia. Yet we urge you, brothers, to do so more and more" (1 Thessalonians 4:9-10).

Continuing his description of Tychicus, Paul then refers to him as "a faithful minister. This describes his relationship to his God. In a television interview a pastor was asked, "Are you the minister of this church?" To which he replied, "No, I am the pastor of this church. My congregation are the ministers. We believe in the priesthood of all believers. When this service is over they will go out to minister in the name of the Lord in the community where they live." I like that! It certainly describes that congregation's relationship to their God.

Paul's final phrase concerning Tychicus, "a fellow servant in the Lord", describes his relationship to both his fellow Christians and to God. No Christian can be an isolated individual even if he stands alone in his community or place of employment. There is always that wonderful and mystical relationship with God, and even though they may appear far away, there is still that relationship with other Christians. And here is an interesting fact. They in turn may be standing alone just where they are valuing their relationship with you.

So let us preserve this wonderful and unique relationship. No, let us do more! Let us nurture and develop this wonderful relationship of beloved brothers and sisters, of faithful ministers and fellow-servants in the Lord – we will never feel lonely if we do!

Colossians 4:17: Archippus

Tell Archippus: "See to it that you complete the work you have received in the Lord."

You will no doubt recall what we said earlier that Archippus was Philemon's
son, and that this reference suggests that he was also the pastor of the church that met in his father's house. When Paul wrote these words he addressed them especially to this one man. How, then, can they help us? Bearing in mind what we said in the *Introduction*, "All Scripture is God breathed and is useful…", although Paul wrote the words and Archippus received them, here is God's word to us, collectively and individually. In other words, God is speaking the words and we must receive them. So God is saying to each one of us, "See to it that you complete the work you have received in the Lord." I rather prefer the *Authorised (King James) Version* of this verse.

"Take heed to the ministry which thou has received in the Lord, that thou fulfil it."

But someone may be saying (in spite of reading the previous "cameo"!), we are not *all* ministers, we do not *all* wear our collars the wrong way round! We do not *all* stand in the pulpit and preach. We may agree with the collar idea and even the pulpit idea, too, but are these really the signs of a minister? For some, admittedly the ministry may include the so-called "dog-collar", and it may mean mounting the pulpit to preach the gospel, but these are only very small aspects of the whole. Yet, you know, some still harbour this false idea – even Christians – concerning the work of the Christian ministry.

Not long after leaving theological college I was approached by a soldier, for the town in which I was ministering was a garrison town. It was near a large army camp in the North of England.

This soldier said to me, "I wish I had your job, it must be smashing."
"Why do you say that?" I asked.

But somehow I knew what the answer was going to be – and I was right! "Well a couple of quick sermons on a Sunday and that's your lot; what an easy life, nothing to do all week."

How wrong he was, yet even committed Christians sometimes share this view. The ministry is more than just a couple of quick Sunday sermons, even with the addition of one or two weekday sermons to take into account And it is also more than one man conducting a service or two in a church. Do you remember the television interview referred to in the previous "cameo"? The pastor had said he was not the minister. "My congregation are the ministers. We believe in the priesthood of all believers." If we, therefore, believe in the priesthood of all believers, then every committed Christian is a minister in the New Testament sense of the word – every committed Christian has a ministry. "When this service is over they (the congregation) will go out to minister in the name of the Lord in the community where they live."

At work or at home, in office, shop or factory, over the garden fence or in the fish and chip shop queue, at school or college, or even in the church fellowship, we are expected as Christians to minister – to be ministers. What we do and say is not only *for* the Lord, but should be *of* the Lord, too. If we believe the Lord has called us into full-time Christian ministry (and bearing in mind what we have just said about the priesthood of all believers, in this sense every committed Christian should be *full-time*), then we must "take heed to the ministry".

Accepting, then, that each of us is a minister with a particular ministry, let us look at it, examine it, study it, make sure it is of the Lord, that it really is His will for us (not the other way around) that makes us do and say those things in His name, whatever "those things" might be. Then, having taken heed to that ministry, assuring ourselves through the Holy Spirit that we are fully committed in His service, we go on to fulfil it. This, of course, means we go on to do our very best, because we do it all for the Lord. As our faces differ, so might the ministries to which we have been called. We said in our very first "cameo", and we repeat it now here in our last, that there will be no doubt in our minds when God does call us to what He wants us to do for Him. His call is personal, and may vary greatly from our neighbour's calling. We must realise, therefore, that whilst we may receive a calling very different from our neighbour or even our partner in life, this may not always be the case, of course. I personally thank God that through the years of ministry to which I have been called, the Lord has graciously called my partner into that same ministry, and God has richly blessed it. Even now in retirement we are still working together in the Lord's work. But, whatever ministry we may have received in the Lord, if it is of Him it is important, it has its place and God will bless it.

We cannot all be pastors of local churches, which is just as well if we stop to think about it for a moment! Paul is here saying to the Colossians, and God is here saying to us just wherever we are, that whatever work the Lord has given us to do for Him we must do it to the very best of our ability.

However humble it might be, if it is *for* the Lord and *of* the Lord it is important.

Permit me just one final illustration from the Christian hotel from which we have now retired. I can still recall the guest, a little elderly gentleman from Cardiff in South Wales, who every morning went around the lounge before breakfast, and around the dining room after breakfast, shaking hands with all the other guests, with a simple "God bless you, sister" or "God bless you, brother" each time. It was a very nice gesture even if a little unusual, so I asked him why he did it.

This was his reply. "You see, Mr. Wheadon, back home in my church I'm the door-keeper. I'm not much good at anything else, but I make sure everybody gets a handshake and a welcome. I find it hard to get out of the habit when I am on holiday. I hope you don't mind."

And of course I didn't.

"See to it that you complete the work you have received in the Lord," we are told. Or, to use the

Authorised (King James) Version of this verse, "Take heed to the ministry which thou hast received in the Lord, that thou fulfil it" – even the ministry of the handshake; *especially* the ministry of the handshake.

Conclusion

Conclusion

Yes, the church today desperately needs the message of Colossians. There is no place for "religious tolerance" with its attendant danger of "diluting the faith". As Christians, it is important that we should take our responsibilities seriously, never allowing non-Christian beliefs and practices to creep into our churches thereby weakening our witness and influence. We have a *responsibility* to present a true picture of Christ to the world, and I trust the "cameos" in this small booklet will help in some way to this end, having taken these selected verses from Colossians in an attempt to make the Bible relevant to this present age.

Jesus Himself has a word to say to us on this matter of *responsibility*. Speaking to His disciples – and we must not forget that we are His disciples today, so He is speaking to us also – Jesus reminded them, and now reminds us, that when people hear us speaking in His name it is as if He Himself is speaking. Obversely, when we reject Jesus by "religious tolerance" and by "diluting the faith", we are presenting a false picture of Christ to the world. Jesus said, "He who listens to you listens to me: he who rejects you rejects me; but he who rejects me rejects him who sent me" (Luke 10:16).

What a *responsibility* is ours, for the sad fact is that we ourselves can reject Jesus by our words and actions, and cause others to reject Him, also. Think of it for a moment. It is in my power to present a false picture of Christ. It is in your power, too. How very careful we must be when we speak in His name.

Frequently it has been said that some of the greatest sermons ever preached have been those with no actual words spoken. A life *lived* for Jesus "speaks" volumes! Without altering the meaning of God's Word in any way, we could also say, "He who sees you sees Jesus." So not only the words that we speak, but also the life that we live, should be a reflection of Jesus Christ, and our *responsibility* is to see that they are a *true* reflection by not allowing "religious tolerance" to creep into *our* church, by not "diluting the faith" in *our* ministry.

May the message of Colossians, so desperately needed in the Church today, become through these "cameos", a *personal* message to each one of us, as the Bible is made relevant to the present age. And may the prayers of Epaphras, as recorded by Paul in Colossians 4:12, be answered in each of us, that we "may stand firm in all the will of God, matured and fully assured".

———————————————

Also on Colossians

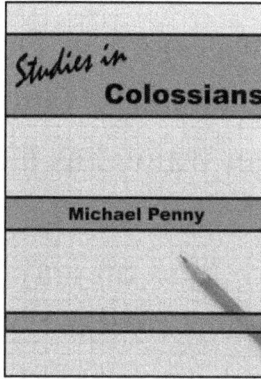

Studies in Colossians
Michael Penny

Details of this book, and the ones on the following pages, can be seen on **www.obt.org.uk** They can be ordered from that website and also from

The Open Bible Trust,
Fordland Mount, Upper Basildon,
Reading, RG8 8LU, UK.

They are also avaialble as eBooks from Amazon and Apple, and as KDP paperbacks from Amazon.

About the author

Denis Wheadon was born in Dorset in 1931. He was educated at Foster's Grammar School in Sherborne and later trained as a commercial artist and industrial illustrator. He did his national service in the RAF, and on leaving worked in the education department of the UK Atomic Energy Authority, before going to theological college and being ordained in 1954. He was a regular broadcaster on Two Counties Radio with Pause Awhile from 1983-1991, and owned a Christian Hotel with a daily Christian ministry.

Other works by Denis Wheadon include:

The Land of Spiritual Experience – Deuteronomy
In the Beginning – Genesis 1
In My Father's House – John 13-17
A Full Reward – Ruth

Details of these can be seen on

www.obt.org.uk

The Land of Spiritual Experience
Meditations in Deuteronomy
Denis Wheadon

In the Beginning
A Study of Genesis 1:1-5
Denis A Wheadon

In My Father's House
Meditations from John chapters 13-17
Denis Wheadon

A Full Reward
Meditations from The Book of Ruth
Denis Wheadon

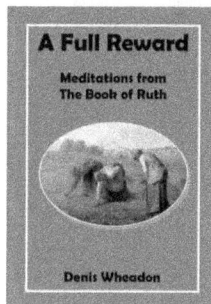

Details of these books can be seen on
www.obt.org.uk
They can be ordered from that website and also from

The Open Bible Trust,
Fordland Mount, Upper Basildon,
Reading, RG8 8LU, UK.

They are also avaialble as eBooks from Amazon and Apple, and as KDP paperbacks from Amazon.

About this book

Cameos in Colossians
Meditations from
Paul's Letter to the Colossians

As the title suggest, selected verses are taken from Paul's letter to the Colossians. These *cameos* aim to meet personal needs in Christians today and seek to make the Bible relevant to the present age of grace in which we live.

In another of his letters, Paul tells us that "All Scripture is God-breathed and is useful for teaching, rebuking, correcting and training in righteousness, so that the man of God may be thoroughly equipped for every good work" (2 Timothy 3:16-17).

This being the case, what lessons can be learnt from Colossians which are of profit and value to us living in the 21st C? In this publication the author places before the reader, in the form of cameos, a few such lessons.

www.ingramcontent.com/pod-product-compliance
Lightning Source LLC
Chambersburg PA
CBHW070524030426
42337CB00016B/2092